save the . . .
POLAR BEARS

by **Christine Taylor-Butler**
with an introduction
by **Chelsea Clinton**

PHILOMEL

Dedicated to all the kids who love this planet

as much as I do. Together we can make a difference.

PHILOMEL BOOKS
An imprint of Penguin Random House LLC, New York

First published in the United States of America by Philomel Books,
an imprint of Penguin Random House LLC, 2023

Text copyright © 2023 by Chelsea Clinton

Photo credits: page 2: © vaclav/Adobe Stock; page 5: © st_iv/Adobe Stock; page 10:
© aussieanouk/Adobe Stock; page 13: © Adrian Niculcea/Adobe Stock; page 16:
© Uryadnikov Sergey/Adobe Stock; page 20: hlxandr/Adobe Stock; page 25: © Cloudtail/
Adobe Stock; page 28: © eplisterra/Adobe Stock; page 36: © Gabrielle/Adobe Stock;
page 41: © Photocreo Bednarek/Adobe Stock; page 48: © wustrowk/Adobe Stock;
page 52: © Asmus Koefoed/Adobe Stock; page 59: © Commander Eric Davis/NOAA
Photo Library; page 61: © Christine Taylor-Butler; page 65: © Thomas W. Johansen/NASA;
page 68: © elizalebedewa/Adobe Stock

Philomel Books is a registered trademark of Penguin Random House LLC.

Visit us online at penguinrandomhouse.com.

Library of Congress Cataloging-in-Publication Data is available.

Printed in the United States of America

ISBN 9780593404027 (hardcover)
ISBN 9780593404034 (paperback)

1st Printing

LSCC

Edited by Talia Benamy and Jill Santopolo • Design by Lily Qian
Text set in Calisto MT Pro

save the . . .

save the . . .
BLUE WHALES

save the . . .
ELEPHANTS

save the . . .
FROGS

save the . . .
GIRAFFES

save the . . .
GORILLAS

save the . . .
LIONS

save the . . .
POLAR BEARS

save the . . .
TIGERS

save the . . .
WHALE SHARKS

Dear Reader,

When I was around your age, my favorite animals were dinosaurs and elephants. I wanted to know everything I could about triceratopses, stegosauruses and other dinosaurs that had roamed our earth millions of years ago. Elephants, though, captured my curiosity and my heart. The more I learned about the largest animals on land today, the more I wanted to do to help keep them and other endangered species safe forever.

So I joined organizations working around the world to support endangered species and went to our local zoo to learn more about conservation efforts close to home (thanks to my parents and grandparents). I tried to learn as much as I could about how we can ensure animals and plants don't go extinct like the dinosaurs, especially since it's the choices that we're making that pose the greatest threat to their lives today.

The choices we make don't have to be huge to make

a real difference. When I was in elementary school, I used to cut up the plastic rings around six-packs of soda, glue them to brightly colored construction paper (purple was my favorite) and hand them out to whomever would take one in a one-girl campaign to raise awareness about the dangers that plastic six-pack rings posed to marine wildlife around the world. I learned about that from a book—*50 Simple Things Kids Can Do to Save the Earth*—which helped me understand that you're never too young to make a difference and that we all can change the world. I hope that this book will inform and inspire you to help save this and other endangered species. There are tens of thousands of species that are currently under threat, with more added every year. We have the power to save those species, and with your help, we can.

Sincerely,

Chelsea Clinton

save the . . .
POLAR BEARS

CONTENTS

THE COLDEST HABITAT ON EARTH

What is the largest land predator on Earth? You might be tempted to say an elephant. Elephants are the largest animal living on land, but they don't prey on other animals. They're strictly vegetarians. If you thought of grizzly bears, you'd be getting warmer, even if the place you'd need to search is so cold that grizzlies couldn't survive there. Here's a hint: the largest land predator spends a lot of time hunting and blending in with the snow. If that last clue makes you think of a polar bear, you'd be right. To find one in the wild, you'll have to travel to one of the coldest places on Earth.

Home on Arctic Ice

The scientific name for polar bears is *Ursus maritimus*. That's a Latin phrase meaning "sea bear." They're the only bear on Earth considered to be a marine mammal. You might ask,

A polar bear in Svalbard, Norway.

"Don't marine mammals, like whales, live in the water?" Actually, yes. But polar bears are an exception. Polar bears evolved from grizzly bears almost 300,000 years ago. Over time, they evolved to live in places much too harsh for most of their distant cousins. Unlike grizzly bears, which live and hunt on land, polar bears depend on big blocks of sea ice for their survival. The ice is where they spend most of their lives, traveling long distances and hunting for food. In the winter, the sea ice is attached to the land. But in the summer, the heat causes a lot of it to break up and float away, sometimes with polar bears still on it!

Scientists estimate there are about 26,000 polar bears living in the wild. There may be more. Up to 80 percent of wild polar bears live in northern Canada. But they are also found in four other places: Russia, Alaska in the United States, Greenland (which is part of Denmark), and Svalbard in Norway. All of these places are near the North Pole, where the climate is brutal. The sun shines twenty-four hours a day in summer, but the temperature is still freezing. It only reaches 32°F. And then from October to early March the polar region is cloaked in total darkness. In those winter months, the temperature can drop as low as -40°F. In this land, the air is cold and dry. The winds can be harsh. It is so cold, no trees grow there. Even so, it's the perfect place for polar bears to make a home for themselves and their cubs.

Until 2022, most scientists knew about nineteen populations of polar bears. Think of each population as a group or neighborhood of bears that live within a territory but occasionally run into bears from other groups. Each territory is known as a home range. It can be as small as 20,000 square miles and as large as 135,000 square miles. Sometimes a home range stretches across more than one country because polar bears follow the movement of sea ice. By grouping the bears into populations, scientists can study and track them.

Those nineteen populations of polar bears

A polar bear standing on sea ice.

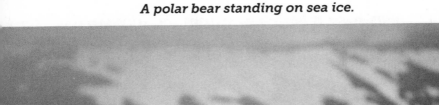

live on or near sea ice in the Arctic region. Sea ice is not the same in every part of that region. Scientists have divided the ice into four types. For example, five polar bear populations live near seasonal ice located in central and eastern Canada. In that region, all of the ice melts each summer. The bears come ashore until the ice forms again in the winter.

Polar basin divergent ice forms in the waters that stretch west from Alaska to Norway. Ocean currents push this ice away from the shore in the summer. That leaves a gap of water between the shore and the ice. Five polar bear populations live in this area. Some bears move to land until winter ice returns. Others swim to reach the ice.

Polar basin convergent ice forms in the waters near eastern Greenland and the Beaufort Sea. The ice is available all year long, but a lot of it has floated from other parts of the Arctic. Two polar bear populations live in this region.

The fourth type of ice is archipelago ice. It is found near the chain of islands north of Canada and Greenland. This area is covered by sea ice all year long. Six polar bear populations live in this region.

The nineteenth polar bear population doesn't live in any of those four ice regions. These polar bears live in the Arctic Basin, which is so remote that scientists can't easily go there to count them.

In 2022, scientists revealed a huge surprise. A new polar bear population had been found in southeast Greenland! With the help of the Inuit and their hand-drawn maps, scientists were able to track the animals for seven years before telling the public about them. That brought the total number of populations to twenty! Those polar bears lived on land so remote, they had not crossed paths with any other groups of polar bears for hundreds of years.

Of the twenty polar bear populations, scientists aren't sure how bears are doing in half of those groups. Those polar bears live in the most extreme parts of northern Russia and Greenland. The land is so remote that there are no roads for cars or safe places to land a small plane. Scientists have to take their best guess based on what they can see when they fly over the area.

A Meal of Seals

Polar bears are apex predators. That means they're at the top of the Arctic food chain and have no natural enemies. Other bears, such as grizzly bears, are omnivores. They eat a variety of foods such as meats, grasses, nuts, and berries. In contrast, polar bears are mostly carnivores, which is another way of saying they are meat-eaters. If they can't find the food they really want, they might eat eggs, rodents, birds, or dead animals. In zoos, they might also eat vegetables and fruit. But polar bear bodies need quite a lot of fuel, and those foods don't provide enough of the right nutrition.

What is a polar bear's favorite meal? Ringed seals! A polar bear's body depends on blubber, or fat, instead of meat. One ringed seal contains all the blubber a polar bear needs to survive for up to eleven days. Of course polar bears can eat other types of seals too. But ringed seals are smaller, and there are more than 2 million of them living in the Arctic. That provides plenty of food for a hungry polar bear to find. A polar

A seal peeks out of a breathing hole near her pup.

bear tries to eat about four pounds of fat each day. If food is plentiful, though, polar bears can eat as much as one hundred pounds in a single day. That helps them store enough fuel for the winter months.

But hunting seals is not easy. Here's how it works: Seals depend on Arctic sea ice to survive too. They use the ice for rest when they're not hunting underwater. Seals are fast in the water but slow on ice. That allows polar bears to sneak up on the seals and pounce to grab them before they can escape. But what happens if the seal is under the ice? That's no problem for a hungry polar bear. Seals need to breathe just like other mammals, so they come up for air every five to fifteen minutes. They use their sharp claws to create breathing holes in the ice to do just that.

Polar bears know this. They use their excellent sense of smell to find the nearest holes. Then they lie very still and wait for a seal to pop its head up to the surface. It may take a few hours or even a few days for a seal to swim back to a specific breathing hole. It's a good thing that hungry polar bears are very patient! Walking uses up thirteen times more energy than resting for polar bears. So waiting around a breathing hole for food to pop up is a more efficient use of their resources. Even with these skills, hunts are successful less than 10 percent of the time.

Baby seals are easier to catch. Polar bears look for snow-covered dens where mother seals have hidden their pups while they search for food. The dens are built on top of the sea ice. Once polar bears pick up the scent of the pups, they dig through the ice and snow to grab their prize.

Long-Distance Swimmers!

We've already learned that sometimes sea ice doesn't stay in one place. It can break off from shore and float away. So what happens if the seals are far from shore, or if there isn't enough sea ice to walk across? No problem!

Polar bears are very determined hunters. Even if they're not as fast as seals, polar bears can still swim up to six miles per hour to get to another section of ice. That's much faster than an average human can swim. And polar bears can swim much farther than humans can. Some have been seen swimming for almost sixty miles without resting. They can hold their breath for more than a minute underwater, but they mostly swim by dog-paddling with their heads above water. All in a day's work for these large marine mammals!

Polar bears are excellent swimmers.

2

TRANSPARENT SEA BEARS

Raising Cubs Is Hard Work!

Polar bears are mostly solitary, but there are a few times when you can find many polar bears hanging out together. For example, when there's a lot of food to share, like when the carcass of a dead whale washes up on the shore. When that happens, several polar bears might join in the feast.

Another time that polar bears gather is in the spring or summer, when males and females will temporarily get together to start a family. A female only gives birth every two years. What's more, she'll only give birth in the winter. Here's how that works.

Unlike other animals, a female polar bear doesn't get pregnant right after she mates. Her eggs are fertilized, but they won't develop inside her until fall or early winter after she's done hunting and gaining weight. When she's ready, she'll dig a deep den in the ice and snow. Some scientists call this a maternity den, much like hospitals have maternity wards where human mothers give birth. A polar bear can't put her maternity den just anywhere. The snow has to be soft enough to tunnel into but deep enough to hide herself and her cubs. The perfect place for a den is in a snow drift or deep slope of snow on land or on sea ice.

A polar bear peeks out of a snow den.

The tunnels stretch as deep as three to nine feet below the surface. The actual den can be as large as eighty square feet. That's the size of a small bedroom in a human home. The den is smart engineering on the part of a polar bear. Outside the den, Arctic winter temperatures can drop as low as -40°F. But inside the den, the temperature will stay closer to 32°F.

Air trapped in the layers of snow or ice acts as insulation.

Once the mother is inside her temporary home, she will go into a deep sleep. You might sleep for eight hours at night, but not a pregnant polar bear. Her heartbeat will slow and she'll rest for three months while her babies develop inside her body. When you go into a deep sleep, you might need to wake to go to the bathroom. You would certainly need to go in the morning. But not a female polar bear. She won't urinate or defecate for three months. During that time, she will only wake up if her den is disturbed or when it's time to have her cubs. By the way, only pregnant females do this. Male polar bears and females that are not pregnant will stay active and hunt all winter.

Remember all those seals that polar bears

hunt? A female has to eat enough blubber to stay alive while she waits to give birth and have enough body fat left over to make healthy milk to feed her cubs. By the time she leaves the den, she's lost almost half her weight.

Born Small but Grow Fast!

A polar bear can have up to three babies at a time, but two is the most common number. At birth the cubs weigh about one pound. Compare that to a human baby, which weighs an average of seven and a half pounds at birth. The cubs are born with no teeth. They also don't have much fat or much fur on their bodies to protect them, so they have to stay close to their mother for food and warmth.

Polar bears grow fast drinking only their mother's milk. It's full of protein and contains

35 percent fat to help them pack on the pounds. In comparison, raw cow's milk contains only 4 percent fat. After a few months, polar bear cubs will weigh about twenty-six pounds. Human babies typically grow for a year or more before they reach that weight. A polar bear mother will leave the den in the spring when the cubs are about four months old. They'll follow her as she hunts. Even though they may start eating blubber she brings to them, the cubs will keep drinking their mother's milk for up to two years.

A mother polar bear is quite affectionate. She will cuddle her cubs with her paws or nuzzle them with her nose and mouth. She might even punish her cubs if needed. Her cubs learn how to hunt from watching her. They also run and chase each other for fun and for practice. Sometimes their playful nature poses

A polar bear mother plays with her cub.

a problem. The vibrations from their pouncing and running might alert a ringed seal that predators are near. They might scare one away before their mother can catch it! But their playtime doesn't last long. After two years, the cubs will leave their mother to start their new lives.

Once cubs become adult polar bears, they grow to be huge. Male polar bears can weigh between 550 and 1,760 pounds. The largest bears weigh as much as ten average-sized men combined! Those polar bears can also grow up to ten feet long. You might have trouble telling male and female polar bears apart. The best way to do so is to look at their size. The females are about half the size of the males and weigh between 300 and 650 pounds. Polar bear weight changes throughout the year based on how much food is available. By the way, polar bears live about twenty-five years.

Fat Polar Bears Are Healthier Bears

Remember when we talked about polar bears being mammals? You're a mammal too. It means your body can make its own heat. That's important to keep you healthy when the temperature grows cold. You have a layer of fat on your body to help keep warmth from escaping. Polar bears do too—their blubber—but theirs is much thicker.

Polar bear blubber can be as much as four inches thick and almost half the bear's weight. Blubber serves several important functions. First, it helps keep the polar bear warm when it is swimming in Arctic waters. Oceans can pull heat from a body faster than a living being can make more to replace what is lost. That's why human divers wear a wet suit to protect them when they plan to be in the water for a long time.

Blubber also helps the bear float. Like you, bears need to keep breathing to survive, so their blubber helps them keep their heads above water when they're not diving to catch seals. More importantly, blubber is how polar bears store energy from all those seals they eat.

See-Through Fur

When you look at a polar bear, you see fluffy white fur, right? Can you believe that the individual hairs that make up that fur have no color at all? That's right. Their hairs are transparent. That's another way of saying you can see through them.

There are two layers of fur covering the bear's body. One layer is short and thick. Scientists call this the undercoat. The hairs of the outer fur are long and silky. Scientists call these the guard hairs. Both types of hair are hollow in the center. The hairs are so thin that you would have to magnify them more than two hundred times to see the tube inside. But those hairs serve three important functions.

First, they act as insulation, trapping heat in the hollow tubes to help protect the bear from the cold air.

Second, the hairs act like camouflage, helping polar bears blend in with their surroundings. How does that work? The hollow tubes inside the hairs scatter light waves. That makes the bears appear white to our eyes.

Third, the hairs are water resistant. That's pretty handy since bears spend a lot of time going in and out of ice-cold water in search of food. The bear can easily shake the seawater off when it returns to land.

By the way, if a polar bear's coat looks yellow, it may be stained by seal oil. If it looks green, it's because algae has gotten inside the

A polar bear shakes water from its fur.

hair tubes. That mostly happens when polar
bears are held in captivity. The algae comes
from ponds in their enclosures. Luckily polar
bears molt. They slowly lose all of their hair in
the summer and grow a new coat.

Heat-Absorbing Skin

You might be thinking that a polar bear's skin is white too, right? It's not! Their skin is black. Sunlight can get past the gaps in the hairs on a polar bear's body. The heat energy is absorbed by the black skin and helps the polar bear stay warm. The bad news is that this works so well, polar bears can get too hot in the summer. They sometimes lie down on ice to cool off. In zoos, they need shade and pools of water to stay cool.

Bodies Built for Hunting

Even though polar bears are related to other types of bears, their bodies are narrower and longer. Their faces and necks are longer too. You might think a polar bear is leaning forward when it walks, and you'd be right. Their front legs are shorter than their rear legs.

Polar bears walk about three to four miles per hour. If there are cubs, the mother will walk about one to two miles per hour. Incredibly, if they are chasing an animal on land, they can run twenty-five miles per hour. That's as fast as a horse! But polar bears can only run a short distance. All that running takes a lot of energy and makes the bear overheat. Their bodies were made for catching food on ice instead of land.

What Big Paws They Have!

Polar bears are pretty heavy animals with paws as big as dinner plates. Those big paws allow them to spread their weight over a large surface area. Their webbed toes allow the paws to act as paddles to help polar bears push water and steer when they are swimming.

Polar bears have big paws.

What about walking on slippery sea ice? Polar bear paws are made for that too. The paws are covered with small bumps called papillae. They grip the ice and keep the bear from falling. Clumps of thick fur between their toes keep their paws warm.

But that's not all those paws can do. Polar

bears use smells from their feet to communicate with other bears. Can you believe it? Polar bears can sniff tracks to find other polar bears. A French biotech company known as SPYGEN figured out that it could get DNA from footprints polar bears left in the snow. DNA is the set of building blocks that makes each animal's body slightly unique. That discovery allows scientists to track the movement of individual polar bears without disturbing them.

Claws

Inside those big paws are claws that are two inches long. That's about the length of your pinky finger. The claws help polar bears grab seals and hang on tight. Unlike many other predators, a polar bear has claws that do not retract. That means they are sticking out all the time instead of protected inside the paws when they're not needed. So don't let a polar bear grab you. They might not let go!

The Nose Knows!

Not only can polar bears track other bears, but they use their excellent sense of smell to find food as far as twenty miles away. They can smell a seal's breathing hole through three feet of snow.

Polar bears' noses don't just help them smell— they help them breathe properly too! Their black nose sits at the end of a much longer snout. Think of the snout as a reverse air conditioner for the polar bear. The polar bear breathes in cold, dry Arctic air. The bear's snout warms the air and adds moisture before it reaches the bear's lungs so that the bear can breathe comfortably.

That Head! Those Teeth!

Even though polar bears have better noses than you do, scientists think their eyesight is similar to yours. The only difference is that they have a special layer on their eyes to protect them from harmful ultraviolet (UV) light. Your eyes don't have that layer, which is why doctors suggest you wear sunglasses with UV protection to protect them on sunny days.

Polar bear ears are short and round to keep water out. That's important, since the ice-cold water could freeze and damage them. And hearing? Scientists created tests and discovered that polar bears hear the same sounds in the same range that humans do.

If you were to look inside a polar bear's mouth, you would see forty-two teeth that include canines, incisors, and molars. That's similar to the way your teeth are organized. The canines are used to hold on to prey. The incisors are used to shred meat. The molars can be used for chewing, even though polar bears often swallow large chunks of seal blubber whole. Did you know that polar bear teeth were the same as other bears' teeth until ten thousand years ago? But now, they are much sharper and their canines are much longer.

Digesting All That Blubber

You already know that polar bears have diets that are high in fat. Most animals, including you, could not survive on fat alone. Polar bears can. They eat as much seal blubber as they can and leave the meat behind. Seal blubber provides all the nutrients they need. Their digestive systems can use up to 84 percent of the protein in the blubber and almost all of the fat.

By the way, polar bears don't have to worry about finding fresh drinking water, because their bodies are able to make water from blubber. In fact, a polar bear can make one ounce of water for every ounce of blubber it eats. Why not drink the water in the seas? Polar bears can't do that, and neither can you. Seawater is full of salt. Eating too much salt would make you both sick.

Nocturnal and Quiet

Unlike people, bears are nocturnal. That means they do most of their sleeping during the day and are most active at night. They'll sleep up to eight hours at a time for a total of twenty hours a day. After all, hunting is hard work.

Polar bears are also mostly quiet. Even when

they are together, they don't seem to communicate much. The mothers use grunts and moans when interacting with their cubs. The cubs make bleating noises when they are in distress. Sometimes polar bears make huffs or snorts, especially when they are nervous. The only time scientists have heard polar bears growl or hiss is when they are being aggressive, which is not very often.

One nice thing about polar bears is they don't bother people unless people bother them. Unfortunately, the world's environment is changing fast, and that change is going to hurt polar bears a lot.

3

SAFE, BUT FOR HOW LONG?

For many years, polar bears have been a symbol of power and strength, especially for many cultures that make their homes in Arctic regions. Some local legends tell of ancient polar bears teaching humans how to hunt seals for food. But changes on our planet are putting these amazing bears at risk of disappearing in the future. Scientists don't want that to happen—and we shouldn't either.

There are a lot of organizations working to

A female polar bear crosses sea ice in Norway.

save polar bears. One of the largest is the International Union for Conservation of Nature (IUCN). They monitor the health of our planet and keep a list of living things that are in danger and need our attention. They call it the IUCN Red List of Threatened Species™. IUCN has studied more than 138,000 species so far. Those that are threatened are grouped in seven levels of increasing danger:

Least Concern: These animals are doing well in their habitats and their numbers are steady or increasing.

Near Threatened: These animals are safe for now, but there are signs they may be in trouble in the future.

Vulnerable: These animals are at risk of extinction, but the risk is still low.

Endangered: These animals are at high risk of extinction. Their numbers are falling and they are losing large amounts of their habitats.

Critically Endangered: These animals have the highest risk of extinction in the wild. If we don't take action, these animals may disappear in the future.

Extinct in the Wild: The only places to find

these animals are in captivity, such as in sanctuaries and zoos. They are no longer found in their natural habitats.

Extinct: There are no more animals of this type living on the planet.

Polar bears are listed as Vulnerable on the Red List. That means that they are okay for now, but conditions around the world put them at risk of disappearing. Even so, the Red List doesn't tell the whole story. The list covers all the polar bears on the planet as if they are one group. But remember, there are twenty different populations, and ten are hard to track. So the status of a specific population of polar bears depends on what region you are talking about.

For example, the polar bears in Greenland and Norway are vulnerable, but the polar bears in Russia may be recovering. Scientists are most worried about polar bears in Canada and in the United States. How safe a polar bear is depends on which governments and agencies are working to protect them. For now, the total polar bear population is still healthy. That's the good news. But here's the bad news. Without everyone's help, polar bear populations are estimated to drop more than 30 percent by the year 2050.

You might ask, "If polar bears aren't fully endangered, why do we think they'll disappear in the future?" There are many reasons.

Climate Change

You may have heard of climate change. It's causing major problems for our planet. Why is this happening? One reason is harmful gases called greenhouse gases are staying in Earth's atmosphere longer than they are supposed to. Carbon dioxide is one of them. That's the gas you release when you breathe air out of your lungs. But it's also created when people burn fossil fuels like oil for cars, manufacturing, and heating. Our atmosphere lets in just the right amount of heat from the sun to allow life to exist on Earth. But carbon dioxide builds up in the atmosphere and acts like a blanket. It traps too much heat. That extra heat is causing climates around the world to change. For polar bears, this will create two huge problems in the future.

Shrinking Sea Ice

This is the greatest threat to polar bears. We've learned that polar bears survive best when the weather is cold and there's lots of snow and sea ice. We also learned that Arctic ice allows polar bears to hunt seals efficiently. The problem is the Arctic regions are warming, and changes to those areas are happening at four times the rate of the rest of the world. The short summers are growing longer and hotter, which means the

Melting sea ice makes it harder for polar bears to hunt seals.

sea ice is melting faster than normal. Having no solid ice near land cuts off a lot of polar bears' access to seals. And although polar bears can temporarily eat other types of meat, they really need seal blubber to survive.

So why can't the bears just swim farther to find seals? Good question. We know polar bears are powerful swimmers. But now when sea ice melts, the pieces float farther from land. Have you ever gone swimming in the ocean or a pool? If you have, then you know that swimming uses a lot of your energy. The same is true for polar bears. So swimming longer distances than normal is a problem. Remember, sea ice melts in the summer when polar bear bodies don't have as much blubber to use for energy as they do in the winter when they are fully fed. Sometimes the polar bears use up more energy finding seals than they gain from eating them.

Unlike whales and other types of sea mammals, polar bears can't stay in the water for long periods of time. Without having ice to walk on, the bears have no way to rest. It is possible for the bears to grow tired and drown. Even if they don't tire themselves out while hunting for seals, polar bears have to swim back to shore eventually. It's hardest for females with young cubs to feed, since they can't bring their cubs with them on a long-distance sea hunt.

Shrinking sea ice creates a problem for humans too. Here's an example: In 2019, a group of hungry polar bears moved to shore and invaded the town of Belushya Guba. The town is located on an island near the Russian coast. The polar bears arrived after the ice in the Barents Sea began disappearing. The residents counted up to fifty-two bears in the area. In fact, so many polar bears arrived that there was one polar bear for every thirty-eight people. Nothing frightened these polar bears—not car horns or dogs or threats from humans. Instead, the polar bears ate from garbage people threw away. They walked into buildings and roamed around the town. Even though polar bears rarely kill people, residents were scared to let their children play outside or walk to school. Shooting polar bears was not legal, so the town had to bring in outside help. They hired experts who could give the polar bears medicine that put them to sleep. Afterward, the experts moved the sleeping polar bears away from the town.

And here's the bad news: scientists predict that only a small amount of sea ice will remain in the summer by the year 2040.

Warmer on Land Too

By the way, longer, hotter summers also mean less snow and ice on land too. The warm weather makes it easier for polar bears to overheat and die. Those are also poor conditions for females that need to create underground dens to hibernate and have their cubs. All of this leads to higher rates of starvation and lower birth weights for the cubs. This lowers the chances of the cubs surviving until they can live and hunt on their own. It also makes the cubs targets for predators. Fewer cubs mean fewer polar bears in the future.

Hunting for Sport

While some places like Belushya Guba make hunting polar bears illegal, that's not true everywhere. Even though polar bears are listed as vulnerable, the Canadian government allows hunting for sport to continue. Because most of the world's polar bear populations live in that country, that's where most of the hunting happens. When scientists complained, the Canadian government made a suggestion they thought would help. Hunters could kill only one female for every two males. Right now, there are three male polar bears living in the wild for every female polar bear. Females don't give birth very often, and not all cubs survive, so Canada thought keeping more female polar bears safe would keep the populations stable.

But remember that you can't tell a female polar bear apart from a male polar bear except by size. And hunters use weapons that allow them to kill from a distance. So there is no good way to tell whether the polar bear is male or female until after the bear is injured or dead. So that's not an ideal solution.

On top of that, Canada is made up of individual provinces. A province is a region that makes its own laws and rules in the same way that states make different rules in the United States. Some provinces put limits on hunting to try to keep polar bears from becoming endangered. But is that enough? Not when you consider that almost one thousand polar bears are still hunted and killed around the world each year, mostly in Canada.

And here's another problem with hunting: Many of the hunters in Canada travel from countries like the US, where hunting polar bears is not legal. The hunters want the biggest and strongest bears for trophies. But those are the bears that can swim the farthest to find food and can survive in the harshest conditions. Killing polar bears with the best chances of survival means their genes won't be passed down to the next generation of cubs. The remaining cubs will have a harder time surviving.

Once polars bear are killed, their bodies are sold to make rugs, trophies, and even seat covers in cars. The rugs once sold for up to $20,000 each, but the average price is now closer to $15,000. That's a lot of money for a single bear-skin. But there are plenty of people willing to pay the price to get one.

So who is buying all those skins? Once upon a time it was Japan and the US. But Japan

This polar bear skin is being used as a rug.

stopped buying them. The US made buying polar bear parts illegal when Congress passed the Endangered Species Act of 1973. Now Canada is the only country that allows the sale of polar bear skins. China is their biggest customer. They buy 70 percent of all the polar bear skins available.

Some people argue that hunting should be allowed because there are still plenty of polar bears in the wild. In some parts of Canada, people believe that there are too many bears near Indigenous communities: almost thirteen thousand at one point. There's a problem with that number, though. When sea ice melts, more bears have to move onto the shore. So it may seem as if there are more polar bears than ever when in fact it's the same number of bears all moving closer to humans.

There is an exception for hunting in countries where it is banned. Indigenous communities such as the Inuit have hunted polar bears for food for thousands of years. Their hunts are legal because it is part of their cultural traditions.

Oil and Gas Drilling

Another threat to polar bears comes from oil and gas companies, which often drill in the same Arctic waters that polar bears need for their habitat. Polar bears are sensitive to the vibrations the equipment makes. The noise can force a mother to leave her den before her cubs are ready. One polar bear left her den when activity started as close as seven hundred feet from her den. Oil companies claim they are trying to locate polar bears so they can stay safely away. They do this by flying over the areas they want to explore for drilling. But studies showed that this isn't effective, because dens are hidden under the ice and snow. In addition to drilling noises, trucks and heavy equipment might drive over the dens by accident. Scientists estimate the oil companies miss the true location of polar bears more than 50 percent of the time.

Pollution

Oil spills from drilling can also pollute seawater. The same happens when freighters have accidents that release the oil they are carrying. That oil can travel on ocean currents to polar bear habitats. If that happens, the oil gets trapped in the water that sits in gaps between sea ice, even if the spill was not nearby. Oil is not easy to remove from polar bear and seal bodies. It might make it harder for a polar bear's fur to

A polar bear finds an old oil barrel.

act as insulation against the cold. That causes the bears to use up more energy staying warm. The oil can also cause the bears to get sick.

Because polar bears are the Arctic's top predator, they are affected when other animals are exposed to other types of pollution too. Seals, for instance, eat fish. But if those fish have been poisoned by human trash, pesticides, or other chemicals in the water, then the polar bear will be affected when it eats the seal.

As an apex predator, polar bears keep the environment in balance. Polar bears eat seals, which eat the fish that humans also need to eat. By keeping the seal population from growing too big, polar bears help humans. Also, polar bears eat mostly blubber. That leaves the seal meat for other predators to find and eat. But if the sea ice disappears, polar bears will have to eat other types of animals on land. And more generally, if polar bears struggle to survive because of climate change, it may be a sign that Earth is becoming unhealthy for humans too. The good news is that there are plenty of people working to save the polar bears. Let's find out more about them now.

4

WHO IS HELPING POLAR BEARS?

As you can see, polar bears are an important part of Earth's ecosystem. It will be hard to heal the planet if we don't help polar bears survive. The good news is polar bears are not disappearing yet. But that may not be true for long. To make sure they remain safe, many people and organizations are working to help.

The Polar Bear Specialist Group

The Polar Bear Specialist Group (PBSG) is

a special part of the IUCN that focuses on improving conditions specifically for polar bears. They were created in September 1965, after a meeting of scientists was held in Fairbanks, Alaska. As part of this group's work, up to thirty-five experts provide conservation information to other organizations and governments on how to best help polar bears thrive. They also monitor how well the bears are doing across the Arctic region. They've discovered that at least two of the twenty polar bear populations are increasing. Those two are in Canada. The bad news is that scientists discovered that three other populations in Canada have decreased. So they are sounding the alarm. The hardest part of their job is getting governments to understand that reversing sea ice melting is a global issue. Every country has contributed to the increase in greenhouse gases that threaten polar bear habitats. The PBSG is providing data in the hopes that governments all over the world will combine forces to make changes that will reverse climate change.

Polar Bears International

Polar Bears International is an organization that is solely dedicated to helping polar bears have a future. It conducts research and funds projects all over the world. They make sure scientists have the equipment they need to do their work, because researching polar bear habitats in remote areas is expensive. The equipment allows scientists to study polar bears in their own environments without getting too close. They also have a new program in Churchill, a town in the Canadian province of Manitoba.

The program uses radar to warn the community before polar bears arrive. What's more, Polar Bears International has programs to help kids learn more about polar bears and talk to the scientists who care about them.

Joanna Sulich, Maternity Den Investigator

One of the scientists working with Polar Bears International is Joanna Sulich. She works in Svalbard, Norway, where all of the country's polar bears live. There, she studies how polar bear maternity dens are changing. The islands have more than one environment: fjords, frozen seas, and small land masses. Some spots there are warmer than others. This helps her study the different ways polar bears and their cubs adjust to changes in their environment. She attaches collars with GPS trackers and solar-powered cameras to the polar bears there to keep an eye on them. Sulich and her team proved that climate change is causing bears to weigh hundreds of pounds less than normal. Their findings give other organizations the tools they need to convince governments to take action on climate change.

Dr. Nicholas Pilfold, Tracking Bears from Above

Dr. Nicholas Pilfold shares his knowledge with Polar Bears International too. He's a large carnivore biologist at the San Diego Zoo Wildlife Alliance. Dr. Pilfold focuses on ways to make sure polar bears have everything they need to survive in the wild. This means going into harsh environments and finding ways to track and study polar bears without disturbing them. He flies over the Arctic seas in a helicopter and looks for polar bears in the maze of ice. The scientists he works with use medicine to put the bears to sleep so they can collect hair and blood samples and make sure the bears are doing well. The data is shared with other organizations and governments to help them with their own research.

*Scientists sometimes use a helicopter
to weigh a polar bear.*

San Diego Zoo Wildlife Alliance

In addition to Dr. Pilfold's work, the San Diego Zoo Wildlife Alliance collects polar bear data in other ways. Living in polar regions is best for polar bears. But sometimes that's not possible. Three cubs were adopted by the San Diego Zoo Wildlife Alliance. Chinook was found wandering in Churchill, Manitoba, in 1995. Tatqiq and her brother Kalluk were found in 2001, after their mother was killed by a hunter. All were too young to survive in the wild on their own. So the zoo adopted them. In 2010 the zoo expanded their exhibit to include more information for visitors. It's now called the Conrad Prebys Polar Bear Plunge. Senior zookeepers like Steve Hebert help the public understand how food and shelter are adjusted so the polar bears can thrive in the warm Southern

California climate. The indoor shelters have small saltwater pools that are kept at a cold temperature. Outside, a 130,000-gallon freshwater pool lets visitors see the polar bears swimming up close, and machines dump snow and ice on the ground for them to roll in. Instead of seal blubber, the polar bears eat salmon and fatty

Two polar bears enjoy a snack at the San Diego Zoo. Afterward, a dip in the pool will help them clean their fur.

meats. But their favorite treat? Lard covered in fish oil! The shelters give the scientists a way to observe polar bear behavior up close and share the knowledge with people around the world.

Dr. Stephen Petersen's Glitter Experiment

Dr. Stephen Petersen is the head of conservation at the International Polar Bear Conservation Centre. He had an interesting idea. He wanted to see how stressed out bears became when they were moved to the Assiniboine Park Zoo in Winnipeg, Manitoba. The best way to measure this would be by examining their blood. But taking blood samples from big bears is dangerous. So he fed them glitter. The glitter he used wasn't harmful to animals. Dr. Petersen used colors like green, red, purple, and gold. And what happened next? When the polar bears defecated, the glitter was all over their poop. Giving each bear a different color allowed the researchers to figure out which mound belonged to which polar bear. The samples were frozen and sent to research facilities around the world. The data has helped scientists learn how to better care for polar bears in captivity. It also has helped them learn how polar bears adjust to changing polar environments.

Greenland's Polar Bear Surprise

Working with local populations sometimes leads to great surprises. Do you remember the new polar bear population that was revealed in southern Greenland in 2022? Inuit communities drew maps and gave scientists clues on where to find them. But there was one problem:

based on what scientists had known, polar bears shouldn't be able to live in southern Greenland! It's warmer than more northern regions, and the sea ice only lasts four months each year. How was it possible the bears were surviving the other eight months without seals?

The National Aeronautics and Space Administration (NASA) has a special division that studies ice loss in Greenland. It's called Oceans Melting Greenland (OMG). OMG helped a team of scientists to track the bears. One of those scientists was Dr. Kristin Laidre. She attached radio collars to twenty-seven bears and tracked them for seven years. As it turns out, the bears have a very small home range compared to the other polar bear populations: only a few square miles. They hunt on frozen chunks of glacier ice and cross over

This polar bear hunts on glacial ice in southern Greenland.

mountains. Why does this have scientists so excited? These polar bears adapted to an environment with less sea ice, which might mean other polar bears can too. Even so, that will only happen if we combat climate change to keep all forms of ice from disappearing in the polar regions. But if these bears exist, could there be others? Scientists continue to search for more good news.

Governments Take Action on Hunting

In 1973, Canada, the US, Denmark, Norway, and the Soviet Union signed the Agreement on the Conservation of Polar Bears. Those countries would limit the number of polar bears that could be killed for sport. Hunters could no longer hunt polar bears using planes, helicopters, or motor vehicles. Each of the countries agreed to conduct research and share their data to help manage polar bear populations around the world. Years later, countries realized they also needed to limit how many polar bears Indigenous communities could hunt. In

1994, Denmark limited Indigenous hunts to one hundred fifty polar bears each year. In 2001, the United States limited Indigenous hunts to eighty-five bears per year.

Svalbard is a great success story. Svalbard has lost almost half its sea ice in the last forty years. Even so, the number of polar bears has increased by 20 percent. How? Norway went further than the 1973 agreement rules. They banned all hunting for any reason.

Your Turn!

As you can see, scientists aren't waiting for polar bear populations to be in the most serious trouble to take action. There are many more efforts happening now, and those efforts will go faster if we all work together by doing what we can to help protect our planet and all of its creatures. Remember, a tiny drop of water can make a big ripple in a pond. By helping these efforts, you can make a difference too!

Two polar bear cubs sleeping with their mother.

FUN FACTS ABOUT POLAR BEARS

1. Male polar bears are called boars. Female polar bears are called sows.
2. A group of polar bears is called a sleuth.
3. Polar bears can mate with grizzly bears. The offspring are called "pizzly bears." Some people also call them "grolar bears."
4. The Inuit, who are indigenous to Alaska, northern Canada, Greenland, and Russia, call polar bears nanuq. In Norway, the bears are called isbjørn, which means "ice bear."

5. The oldest known polar bear fossil is about 130,000 years old.

6. Polar bears can survive in outdoor temperatures as low as -40°F.

7. The longest observed swim by a polar bear was nine days.

8. Polar bears are only found north of the equator. None are found in Antarctica.

9. The biggest known polar bear weighed 2,200 pounds and was twelve feet tall.

10. Polar bears travel the longest distances of any four-legged animal.

11. Polar bears do not get good nutrition from vegetables, but carrots can help keep their teeth clean.

12. Polar bears rarely kill people. There have only been twenty fatal polar bear attacks recorded in 144 years.

HOW YOU CAN HELP SAVE THE POLAR BEARS

Now that you know more about polar bears, you're probably thinking of great ways you can help them. Here are some ideas to get you started and help you change the future!

1. Ask adults not to buy products or pelts made from polar bears. Buying and selling those pelts encourages more hunting. Indigenous nations are allowed to sell the skins of the bears they kill, but it's often impossible to know where the pelts come from.

2. Did you know that Polar Bears International has live webcams of polar bears to let you see them in real time? The bears are located on the shores of the Hudson Bay in Canada. The scientists also schedule video chats so that students and teachers can ask questions of scientists working with polar bears all over the Arctic. Those scientists will have information, videos, and suggestions for how to get involved with saving the polar bears you care about. They even have a polar bear tracker that allows you to track where bears are going. And you can learn more about the ringed seals the polar bears depend on for survival. Head to PolarBearsInternational .org to find out more.

3. Take a Tundra Connections virtual field trip. Discovery Education teamed up with Polar Bears International to host virtual field trips. They have a polar bear channel and lots of other activities to keep you busy and learning about polar bears, which you can find at DiscoveryEducation.com/Learn/Tundra -Connections.

4. Reduce dependence on fossil fuels by walking, riding bicycles, or taking public transportation when possible. This reduces the amount of greenhouse gases released into our atmosphere. That will help reduce climate change.

5. Recycle. Climate change happens in part because of all the new products being made. Recycling finds new uses for paper and plastic so we make less of it. That also helps reduce how much trash is thrown into animal habitats. Recycling saves trees needed to protect the environment. This also reduces the effects of global warming.

6. Hold a fundraiser on International Polar Bear Day. It's celebrated on February 27 each year. You can have a yard sale or a bake sale, or open a lemonade stand. Donate the money you make from those to organizations working to help polar bears. The money you raise will help them carry out their important work. More resources will help these organizations save more polar bears.

7. Write letters to your elected officials asking them to stop drilling activities

in the Arctic Refuge waters. The drilling puts nearby maternity dens at risk if the mother is disturbed, and the oil can spill and cause great damage. You can find your representatives at USA.gov/Elected-Officials.

8. Write letters to scientists to let them know how much you appreciate their important work. It's not easy trying to save the planet, and hearing from people lets them know they are doing a good job. You can find many of them at the organizations listed in chapter 4.

9. Most important, tell friends and family members what you've learned about polar bears, and ask them to spread the word. Many people may not know what is happening or how to help. Let your

voice be heard. Sometimes change happens with a single person. Maybe today, that person can be you.

Together we can make the world safer for polar bears and help their numbers increase!

ACKNOWLEDGMENTS

I would like to thank Ken, Alexis, and Olivia for putting up with my endless hours of research and revision. You're the best! To Kim Parham, the best research assistant on the planet. To Christyn Johnson and Whidbey Institute for fueling me with good food and forest land-scapes to get me over the finish line. And to Steve Hebert at the San Diego Zoo for expanding my knowledge on polar bear care and behavior.

REFERENCES

Can Geo Staff. "Animal Facts: Polar Bear." Canadian Geographic: Kids. *Canadian Geographic*, June 6, 2019. canadiangeographic.ca/articles/animal-facts-polar-bear.

Dal, Ray, dir. *Frozen Planet*. Aired 2011–2012; BBC Earth. Narrated by David Attenborough. Accessed April 30, 2022. bbcearth.com/shows/frozen-planet.

Dutfield, Scott. "Polar Bear Guide: Where They're Found, What They Eat, and Why They're Threatened." Discover Wildlife. *BBC Wildlife*, February 25, 2021. discoverwildlife.com/animal-facts/mammals/facts -about-polar-bears.

Fothergill, Alastair and Jeff Wilson, dirs. *Polar Bear*. 2022; Disney+ Original. Narrated by Catherine Keener. disneyplusoriginals.disney.com/movie/polar-bear.

National Geographic Kids UK. "Polar Bear Primary Resource." PDF file. National Geographic Society. Accessed April 30, 2022. natgeokids.com/uk/primary -resource/polar-bear-primary-resource.

Polar Bear Specialist Group. About. IUCN Polar Bear Specialist Group, 2021. Accessed February 21, 2022. iucn-pbsg.org.

"Polar Bears." Bears: Bears in National Parks. National Park Service, US Department of the Interior. Last modified April 5, 2022. nps.gov/subjects/bears/polar -bears.htm.

Polar Bears International. "Welcome to the Exciting World of the Polar Bear." Accessed February 21, 2022. polarbearsinternational.org/polar-bear-facts.

San Diego Zoo Wildlife Alliance. "Polar Bear." Animals and Plants. San Diego Zoo Wildlife Alliance. Accessed February 21, 2022. animals.sandiegozoo.org/animals /polar-bear.

WWF Arctic Programme. "Polar Bear." Wildlife. World Wildlife Fund, 2022. Accessed February 21, 2022. arcticwwf.org/wildlife/polar-bear.

CHRISTINE TAYLOR-BUTLER is the author of more than ninety fiction and nonfiction books and articles for children. A graduate of MIT, she holds degrees in both civil engineering and art & design. She has served as a past literary awards judge for PEN America and for the Society of Midland Authors. She is an inaugural member of steaMG, an alliance of middle grade science fiction authors, and a contributor to STEM Tuesday. She lives in Kansas City with her husband, Ken, and a cat who thinks he's a dog.

Photo by Kecia Y. Stovall

You can visit Christine Taylor-Butler online at
ChristineTaylorButler.com
and follow her on Twitter
@ChristineTB

CHELSEA CLINTON is the author of the #1 *New York Times* bestseller *She Persisted: 13 American Women Who Changed the World*; *She Persisted Around the World: 13 Women Who Changed History*; *She Persisted in Sports: American Olympians Who Changed the Game*; *Don't Let Them Disappear: 12 Endangered Species Across the Globe*; *It's Your World: Get Informed, Get Inspired & Get Going!*; *Start Now!: You Can Make a Difference*; with Hillary Clinton, *Grandma's Gardens* and *The Book of Gutsy Women: Favorite Stories of Courage and Resilience*; and, with Devi Sridhar, *Governing Global Health: Who Runs the World and Why?* She is also the Vice Chair of the Clinton Foundation, where she works on many initiatives, including those that help empower the next generation of leaders. She lives in New York City with her husband, Marc, their children and their dog, Soren.

You can follow Chelsea Clinton on Twitter
@ChelseaClinton
or on Facebook at
Facebook.com/ChelseaClinton

DON'T MISS MORE BOOKS IN THE

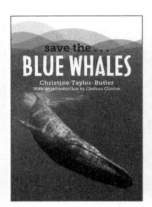

save the . . .
BLUE WHALES
Christine Taylor-Butler
With an introduction by Chelsea Clinton

save the . . .
ELEPHANTS
Sarah L. Thomson
With an introduction by Chelsea Clinton

save the . . .
FROGS
Sarah L. Thomson
With an introduction by Chelsea Clinton

save the . . .
LIONS
Sarah L. Thomson
With an introduction by Chelsea Clinton

save the . . .
POLAR BEARS
Christine Taylor-Butler
With an introduction by Chelsea Clinton